SASKATCHEWAN
JOURNEY ACROSS CANADA

Harry Beckett

The Rourke Book Co., Inc.
Vero Beach, Florida 32964

Harry Beckett M.A. (Cambridge), M. Ed. (Toronto), Dip. Ed. (Hull, England) has taught at the elementary and high school levels in England, Canada, France, and Germany. He has also travelled widely for a tour operator and a major book company.

Edited by Laura Edlund
Laura Edlund received her B.A. in English literature from the University of Toronto and studied Writing for Multimedia and Book Editing and Design at Centennial College. She has been an editor since 1986 and a traveller always.

ACKNOWLEDGMENTS
For photographs: Geovisuals (Kitchener, Ontario), The Canadian Tourism Commission and its photographers.
For reference: *The Canadian Encyclopedia, Encarta 1997, The Canadian Global Almanac, Symbols of Canada. Canadian Heritage*, Reproduced with the permission of the Minister of Public Works and Government Services Canada, 1997.
For maps: Promo-Grafx of Collingwood, Ont., Canada.

Library of Congress Cataloging-in-Publication Data

Beckett, Harry. 1936 -
    Saskatchewan / by Harry Beckett.
       p. cm. — (Journey across Canada)
    Includes index.
    Summary: Describes the geography, weather, history, industries and major cities of the central province known as Canada's breadbasket.
    ISBN 1-55916-204-X
    1. Saskatchewan—Juvenile literature. [1. Saskatchewan.] I. Title.
II. Series: Beckett, Harry 1936-   Journey across Canada.
F1071.4.B43 1997   97-12866
971.24—dc21   CIP
                                  AC

Printed in the USA

TABLE OF CONTENTS

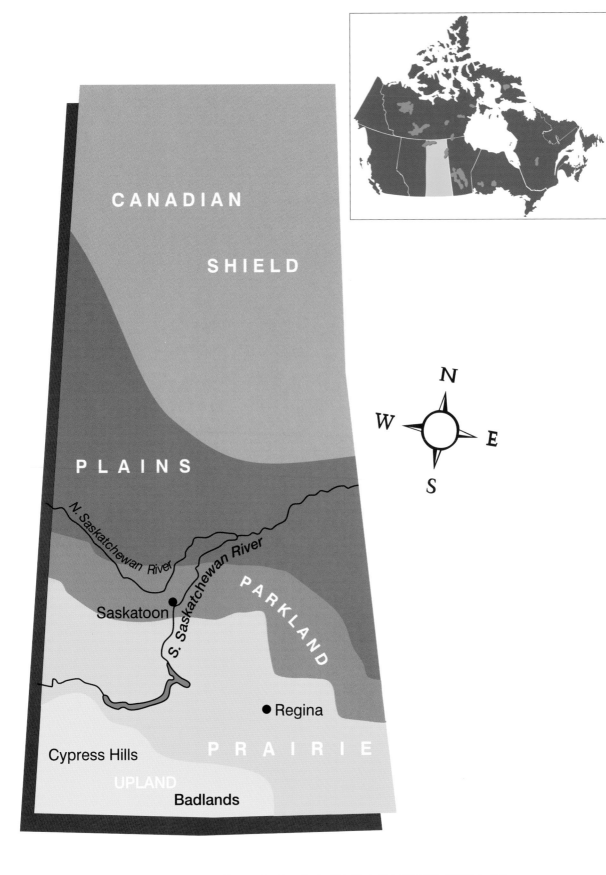

CANADIAN

SHIELD

PLAINS

N. Saskatchewan River

S. Saskatchewan River

PARKLAND

Saskatoon

● Regina

PRAIRIE

Cypress Hills

UPLAND

Badlands

N
W   E
S

PROVINCE OF SASKATCHEWAN

Chapter One

SIZE AND LOCATION

Saskatchewan is the only province that does not have a geographic feature—such as a river, mountain range, or shoreline—as a boundary. It was a district of the Northwest Territories until it became a province in 1905.

The province lies near the centre of Canada, between Alberta to the west and Manitoba to the east. Its southern neighbours are the states of Montana and North Dakota, and it borders the Northwest Territories to the north.

Saskatchewan, Canada's fifth biggest province, is 652 330 square kilometres (251 884 square miles) in area. The population in 1991 was 988 928.

"Saskatchewan" is a Native word meaning "swiftly flowing river."

Find out more...

• The United States-Canada border lies on the 49th parallel.
• The Northwest Territories-Saskatchewan border lies on the 60th parallel.

5

Chapter Two

GEOGRAPHY: LAND AND WATER

Saskatchewan is one of the three **Prairie** (PRARE ee) provinces. There are prairies in the south and the **Canadian Shield** (kuh NAY dee un SHEELD) in the north.

The far north of the Shield is swampy or **permafrost** (PUR muh frost). Further south, the low, rocky land is covered with forests and lakes.

Southern Saskatchewan is mainly flat, with few trees.

Grain elevators on the rolling land of southwestern Saskatchewan

South of the Shield is the "grain belt," a gently rolling plain of good soil left behind by **glaciers** (GLAY shurz).

The southwest of the province is a higher, rolling plain. The Cypress Hills in the extreme southwest, are the highest land between the Rocky Mountains and Labrador.

Most of the rivers flow to the northeast, towards Hudson Bay, because the land is lower there than in the southwest.

7

Chapter Three

WHAT IS THE WEATHER LIKE?

Saskatchewan has very cold winters and hot summers. The summers are cooler towards the north. This kind of climate is called a continental climate.

Annual rain and snow is fairly light, with even less in the north. The snowfall is not heavy, but it stays on the ground all winter. Most of the rain falls around harvest time. Farming depends on rainfall and on the melting snows, which vary from year to year. **Droughts** (drowts), floods, snow, and hail can harm the crops.

In the south there are about 150 days without frost. The long days of summer help the crops.

Find out more...

• Saskatchewan has a continental climate because it is away from ocean influences.

• Midale and Yellowgrass hold the Canadian record for high temperatures, 45°C (113° F).

Winters are cold, but they can be fun at Waskimo Winterfest.

Chapter Four

MAKING A LIVING: HARVESTING THE LAND

Agriculture is Saskatchewan's largest industry. Fur traders came first, but farming was the reason people came to settle.

Saskatchewan is called Canada's breadbasket because it is the largest wheat producer in the country and among the largest in the world. Farms are mostly large, and sales of farm machinery are high.

Half of Saskatchewan is wooded, but forestry is not a major industry. Most of the wood is softwood, which is made into lumber, particle board, plywood, fenceposts, and pulp.

Hunting and fishing are important in the north.

Harvesting grain in Canada's breadbasket

Find out more...

- Wheat production has increased steadily, except in the Depression, in the 1930s, and during other serious droughts.
- Saskatchewan also grows rye, oats, flaxseed, canola, barley, and forage crops.

11

Chapter Five

FROM THE EARLIEST PEOPLES

The original inhabitants of Saskatchewan were **Athapascan** (ath uh PAS kun), **Algonquian** (al GONG kee un), and **Siouan** (SOO un) peoples. European explorers came first to the north looking for furs. Later, in the nineteenth century, farming attracted settlers to the south.

Some settlers arrived on the newly built railway from the east, drawn by offers of cheap land.

A bronze statue of a Native man and a mounted policeman meeting on the prairie

Trading posts like this one at Fort Walsh served the early settlers.

Native peoples were moved to reserves to open
up territory. In 1873, the North-West Mounted
Police was formed to keep the peace after
trouble in the Cypress Hills. Twelve years later, a
Métis (MAY tee) rebellion was ended.

Large-scale immigration stopped with the
Depression of the 1930s. Since then, people have
continued to arrive, but others have left, to fight
in World War II (1939-45) or to find jobs
elsewhere.

Chapter Six

Industry is based on the province's natural products. Mining and gas and oil production have grown quickly since 1950.

Saskatchewan is the world's leading uranium producer and supplies a quarter of the world's potash. It ranks second in Canada in oil production and third in natural gas, with other minerals also important.

Manufacturing has grown slowly, generally because Saskatchewan is far from large markets, and the province's raw materials do not suit manufacturing.

Saskatchewan has a good east-west road and rail network, with spurs north and south.

Towns serve as shipping and trading centres for surrounding farms.

Find out more...

- Mining and oil and gas production are now second to wheat in importance.
- Gold, silver, copper, and zinc are taken from the Shield, and coal and clay from the prairies.

Coal mining with Big Lou, one of the world's largest drag line machines

14

Chapter Seven

IF YOU GO THERE...

You can walk or climb in the Great Sand Hills of the southwest, or fish and canoe in national and provincial parks. Many visitors go to the badlands—dry and dusty hills, weirdly shaped by wind and rain. The many historic sites are symbols of the feelings that locals have for their history.

In almost every community, festivals celebrate Saskatchewan's various peoples. Native peoples hold powwows and the cities of Saskatoon and Regina have major festivals of food, crafts, and music.

The long, cold winters bring communities together to enjoy cross-country skiing, snowmobiling, curling, and ice-hockey. Saskatchewan has produced many famous hockey players.

Young dancer at a powwow at Fort Qu'Appelle

Find out more...

- There are historic sites at Fort Battleford, Fort Walsh, and Batoche.
- Batoche played a role in the Métis Rebellion of 1885.

17

Chapter Eight

MAJOR CITIES

Regina, the capital of Saskatchewan, is the business centre of the wheat-growing prairie. It was built on Wascana Creek, on the route of the Canadian Pacific Railway. The legislature, arts and science centres, and a natural history museum are built around Wascana Lake.

The Royal Canadian Mounted Police has trained in Regina since 1885, when it was called the North-West Mounted Police.

A peaceful oasis in the middle of Regina

Saskatoon on the South Saskatchewan River

Saskatoon, the province's largest city, is a hub of western Canada's rail network in rolling parkland on the South Saskatchewan River. Visitors and locals enjoy the Ukrainian Museum of Canada, the Yevshan Folk-Ballet, and the nearby Wanuskewin Heritage Park, with its buffalo grounds and Native artifacts.

Chapter Nine

SIGNS AND SYMBOLS

The flag has two horizontal bands—green and gold to represent the northern forest and the southern grain fields. The provincial shield is in the upper corner and the flower, opposite. The shield shows a red lion above three gold wheat sheaves on a green field, symbols for agriculture.

The coat of arms shows the shield as well as a lion and white-tailed deer with Native beadwork collars. One bears the Canadian maple leaf and the other, the provincial flower. The beaver represents the North, the fur trade, and the Native people.

The provincial flower is the western red lily, common in meadows and clearings.

The Latin motto means "From many peoples, strength."

Saskatchewan's flag, coat of arms, and flower

GLOSSARY

Algonquian (al GONG kee un) — Native peoples, including Blackfoot and Cree peoples

Athapascan (ath uh PAS kun) — Native peoples, including Chipewyan and Slave peoples

Canadian Shield (kuh NAY dee un SHEELD) — a horseshoe-shaped area of rock covering about half of Canada

drought (drowt) — a long period of dry weather

glacier (GLAY shur) — large mass of ice

Métis (MAY tee) — French, meaning person of mixed blood, especially descending from French and Native ancestry in prairie river valleys

permafrost (PUR muh frost) — ground that is always frozen at, or just below, the surface

Prairies (PRARE eez) — Manitoba, Alberta, and Saskatchewan named for their plains

Siouan (SOO un) — Native peoples, including Assiniboine peoples

At the Buffalo Days Festival, in Wascana Park, Regina

INDEX